PIANO · VOCAL · GUITAR

MEN OF COUNTRY MUSIC

This publication is not for sale in
the E.C. and/or Australia
or New Zealand.

ISBN 0-7935-5946-4

HAL·LEONARD
CORPORATION
7777 W. BLUEMOUND RD. P.O. BOX 13819 MILWAUKEE, WI 53213

Copyright © 1996 by HAL LEONARD CORPORATION
International Copyright Secured   All Rights Reserved

For all works contained herein:
Unauthorized copying, arranging, adapting, recording or public performance is an infringement of copyright.
Infringers are liable under the law.

CONTENTS
Alphabetical by Artist

4 **CLINT BLACK**
Untanglin' My Mind

14 **BROOKS & DUNN**
Boot Scootin' Boogie

18 **GARTH BROOKS**
Ain't Going Down ['Til the Sun Comes Up]

24 **MARK CHESNUTT**
Brother Jukebox

9 **MARK COLLIE**
Three Words, Two Hearts, One Night

28 **EARL THOMAS CONLEY**
Love Out Loud

33 **RODNEY CROWELL**
Above and Beyond

36 **JOE DIFFIE**
Pickup Man

43 **VINCE GILL**
Which Bridge to Cross [Which Bridge to Burn]

48 **VERN GOSDIN**
I Can Tell By the Way You Dance [How You're Gonna Love Me Tonight]

58 **LEE GREENWOOD**
Dixie Road

53 **MERLE HAGGARD**
Twinkle Twinkle Lucky Star

62 **ALAN JACKSON**
Chattahoochee

66 **WAYLON JENNINGS**
Luckenbach, Texas [Back to the Basics of Love]

70 **GEORGE JONES**
She's My Rock

75 **RONNIE MILSAP**
Don't You Ever Get Tired [Of Hurting Me]

80	**JOHN MICHAEL MONTGOMERY**	No Man's Land
84	**GARY MORRIS**	I'll Never Stop Loving You
88	**MICHAEL MARTIN MURPHEY**	What's Forever For
91	**WILLIE NELSON**	Always on My Mind
94	**PAUL OVERSTREET**	Daddy's Come Around
100	**EDDY RAVEN**	Joe Knows How to Live
106	**DAN SEALS**	Big Wheels in the Moonlight
116	**T. G. SHEPPARD**	Party Time
120	**RICKY SKAGGS**	Cajun Moon
124	**DOUG STONE**	I Never Knew Love
130	**GEORGE STRAIT**	You Can't Make a Heart Love Somebody
111	**RANDY TRAVIS**	Before You Kill Us All
134	**TRAVIS TRITT**	Here's a Quarter (Call Someone Who Cares)
140	**RICKY VAN SHELTON**	I'll Leave This World Loving You
156	**STEVE WARINER**	You Can Dream of Me
146	**DON WILLIAMS**	I Believe in You
150	**HANK WILLIAMS, JR. & HANK WILLIAMS**	There's a Tear in My Beer
152	**DWIGHT YOAKAM**	Ain't That Lonely Yet

Clint Black

UNTANGLIN' MY MIND

Words and Music by MERLE HAGGARD
and CLINT BLACK

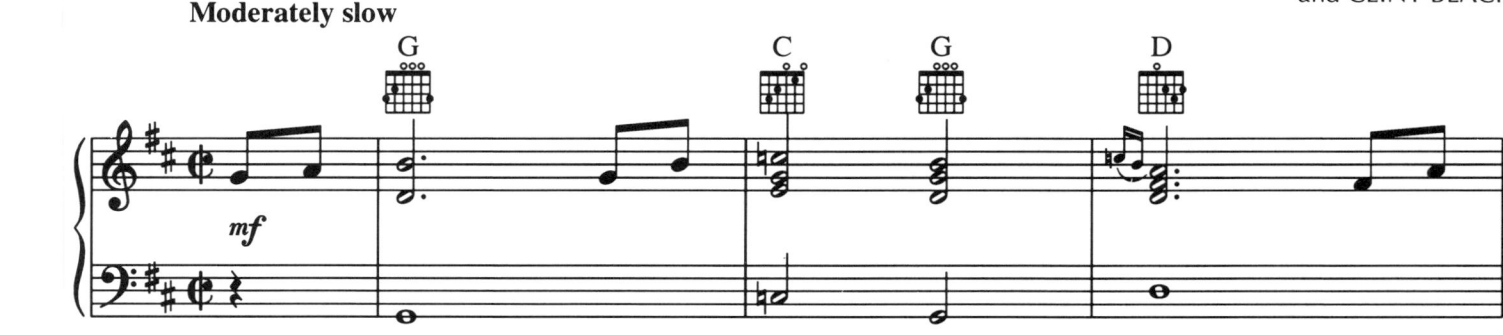

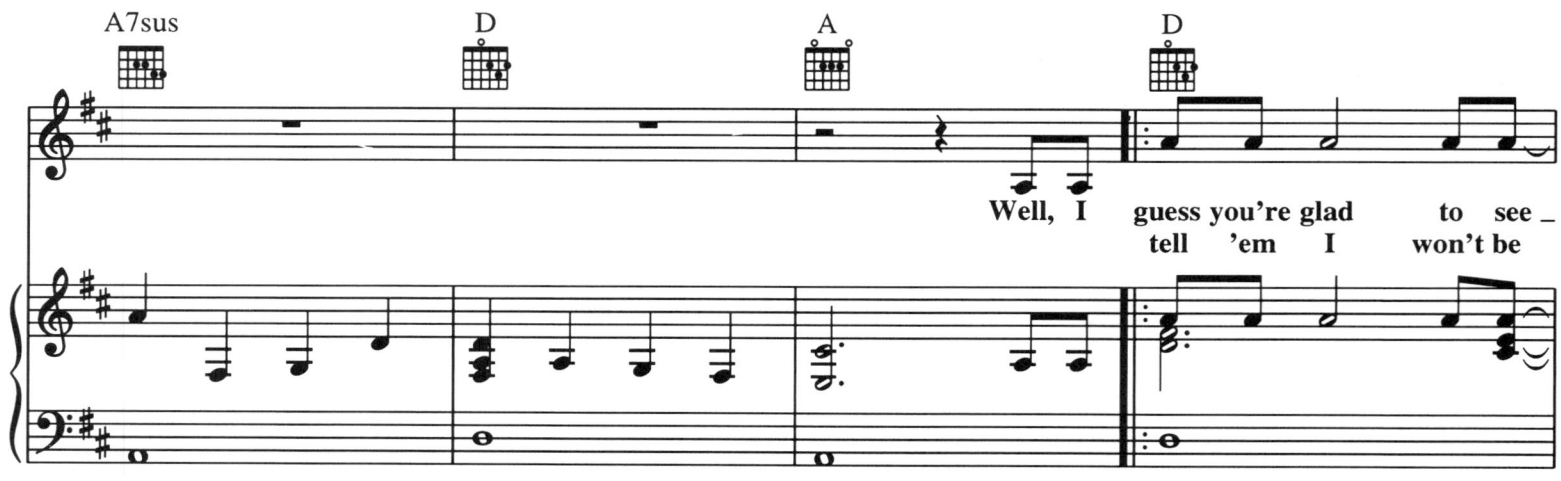
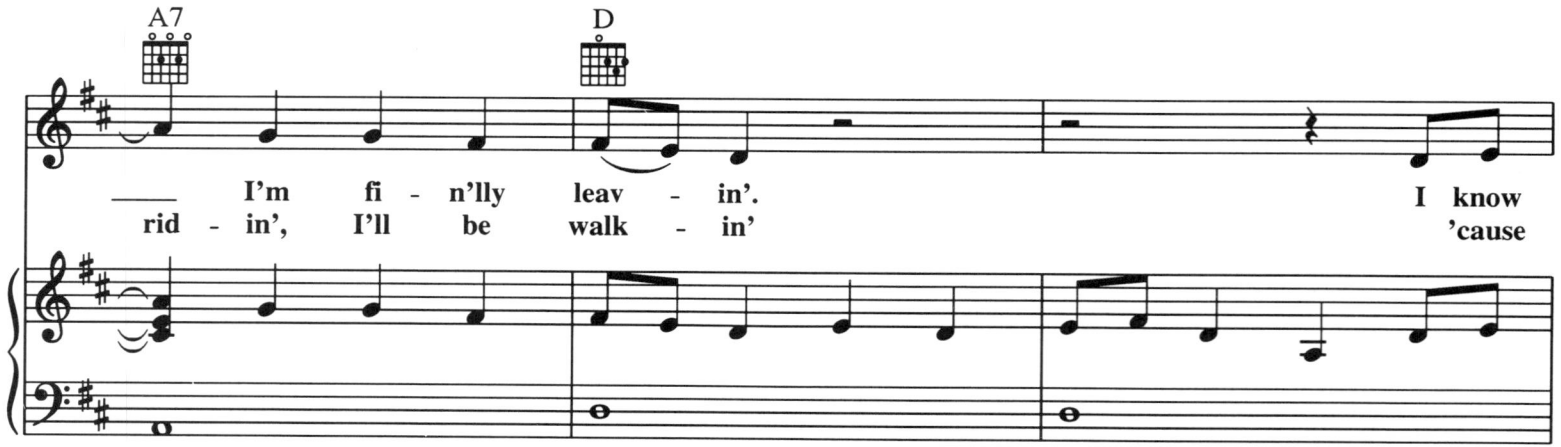

Well, I guess you're glad to see _ I'm fi-n'lly leav-in'. I know
tell 'em I won't be rid-in', I'll be walk-in' 'cause

Copyright © 1994 Sony/ATV Songs LLC, Sierra Mountain Music and Blackened Music
All Rights on behalf of Sony/ATV Songs LLC and Sierra Mountain Music Administered by Sony/ATV Music Publishing, 8 Music Square West, Nashville, TN 37203
International Copyright Secured   All Rights Reserved

THREE WORDS, TWO HEARTS, ONE NIGHT

Mark Collie

Words and Music by MARK COLLIE
and GERRY HOUSE

© Copyright 1995 by MUSIC CORPORATION OF AMERICA, INC., Mark Collie Music and HOUSENOTES MUSIC
All Rights for MARK COLLIE MUSIC Controlled and Administered by MUSIC CORPORATION OF AMERICA, INC.
International Copyright Secured   All Rights Reserved

BROTHER JUKEBOX

Mark Chesnutt

Words and Music by
PAUL CRAFT

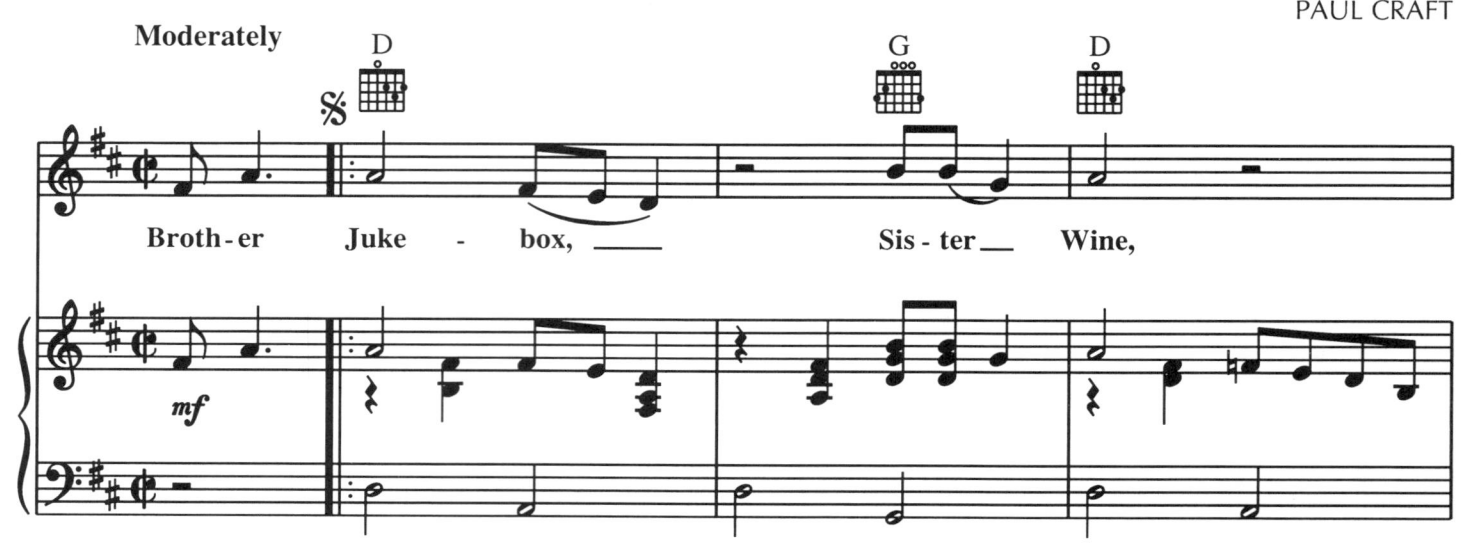

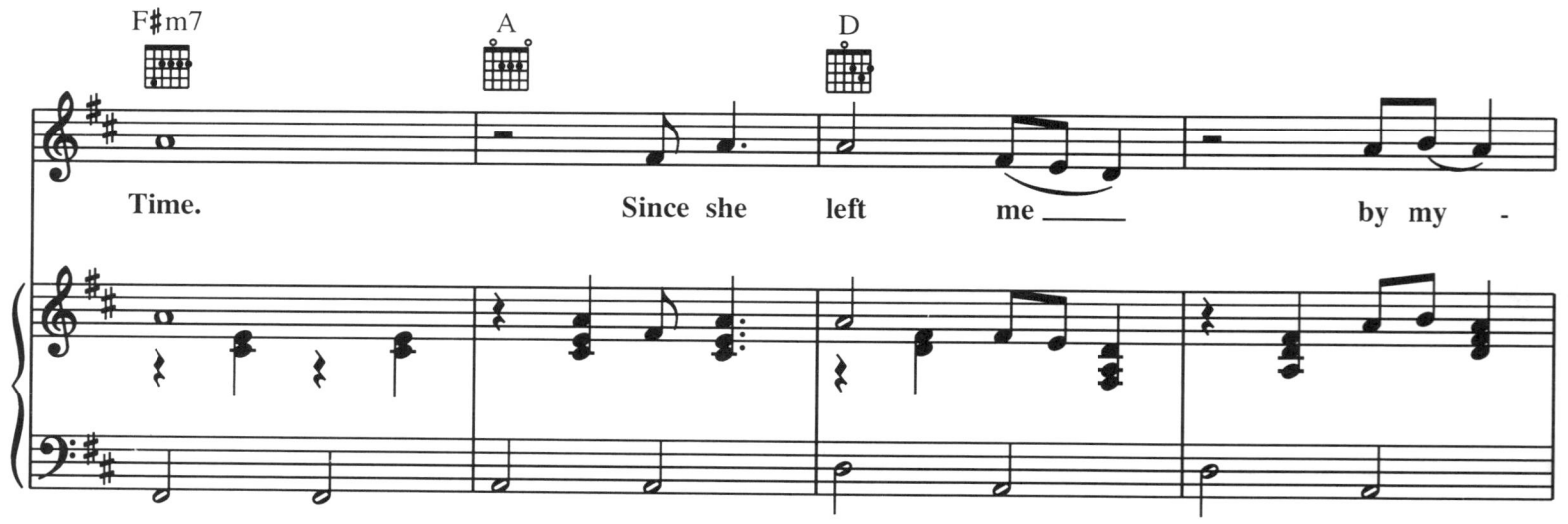

© 1976 SCREEN GEMS-EMI MUSIC INC. and Black Sheep Music
All Rights Controlled and Administered by SCREEN GEMS-EMI MUSIC INC.
All Rights Reserved   International Copyright Secured   Used by Permission

27

ABOVE AND BEYOND

Rodney Crowell

Words and Music by
HARLAN HOWARD

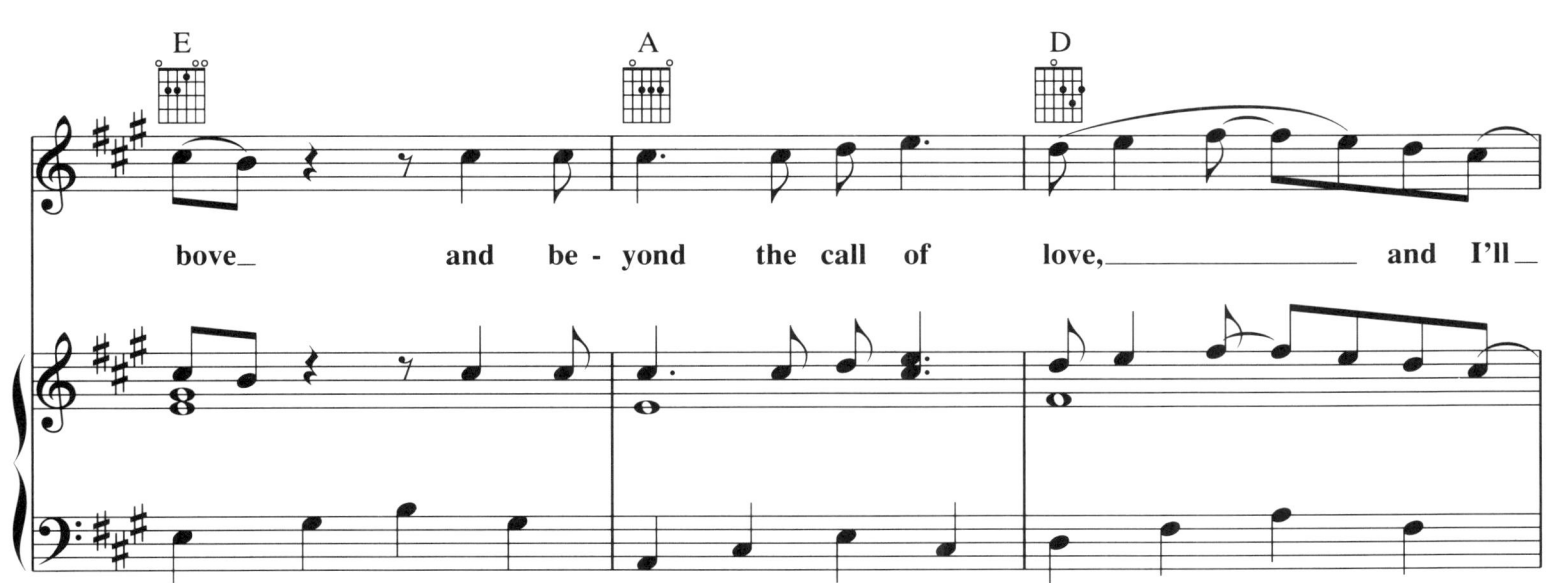

Copyright © 1959 Sony/ATV Songs LLC
Copyright Renewed
All Rights Administered by Sony/ATV Music Publishing, 8 Music Square West, Nashville, TN 37203
International Copyright Secured   All Rights Reserved

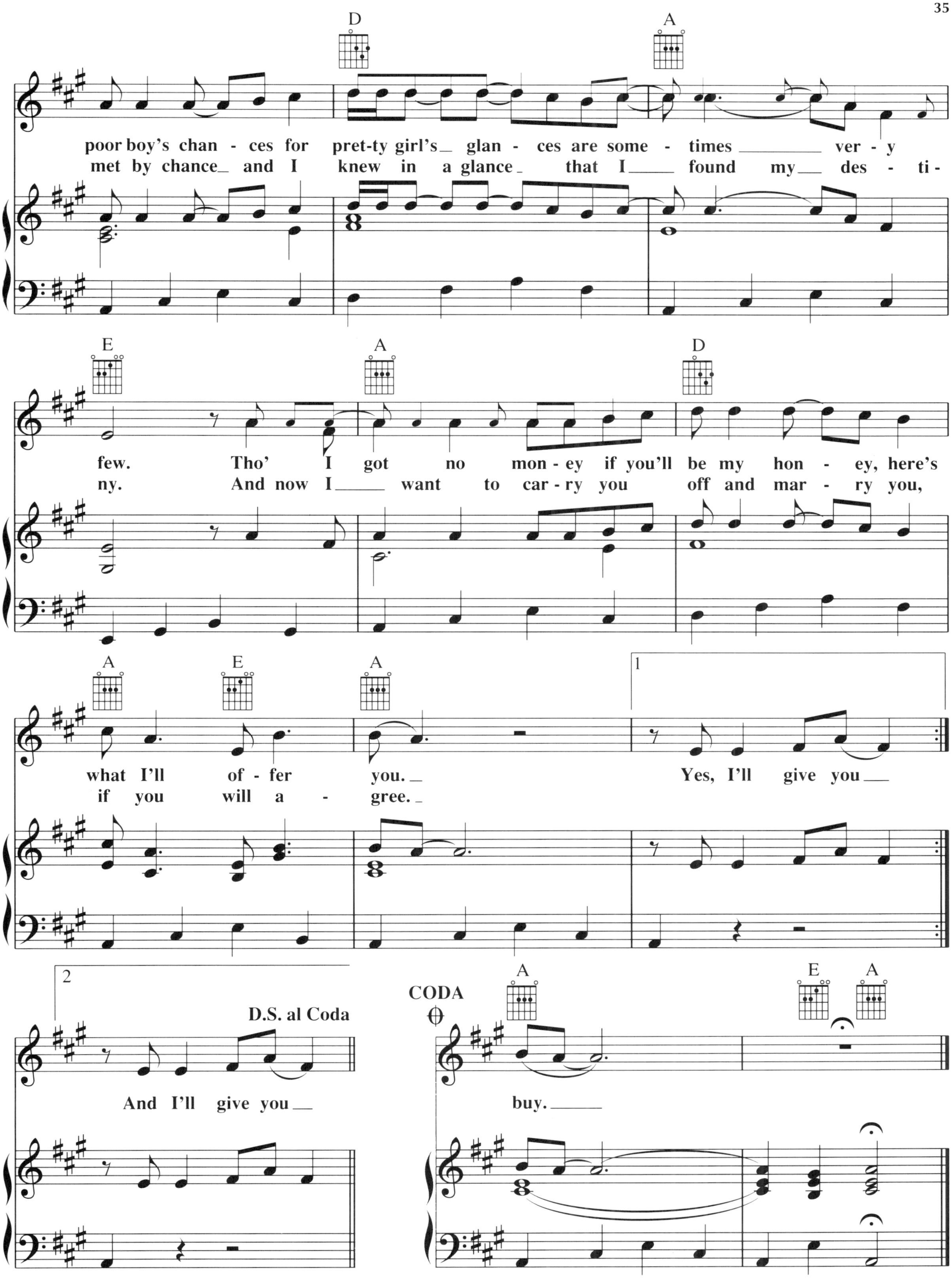
D
A
poor boy's chan - ces for pret-ty girl's glan - ces are some - times very - y
met by chance and I knew in a glance that I found my des - ti -
E
A
D
few. Tho' I got no mon - ey if you'll be my hon - ey, here's
ny. And now I want to car - ry you off and mar - ry you,
A
E
A
1
what I'll of - fer you. Yes, I'll give you
if you will a - gree.
2
D.S. al Coda
And I'll give you
CODA
A
E
A
buy.

Joe Diffie
PICKUP MAN

Words and Music by HOWARD PERDEW
and KERRY KURT PHILLIPS

Copyright © 1994 by Modar Music (BMI), Songwriters Ink (BMI), Emdar Music (ASCAP) and Texas Wedge Music (ASCAP)
International Copyright Secured   All Rights Reserved

42

Vince Gill

WHICH BRIDGE TO CROSS
(WHICH BRIDGE TO BURN)

Words and Music by BILL ANDERSON
and VINCE GILL

Copyright © 1994 Sony/ATV Songs LLC and Benefit Music
All Rights on behalf of Sony/ATV Songs LLC Administered by Sony/ATV Music Publishing, 8 Music Square West, Nashville, TN 37203
International Copyright Secured   All Rights Reserved

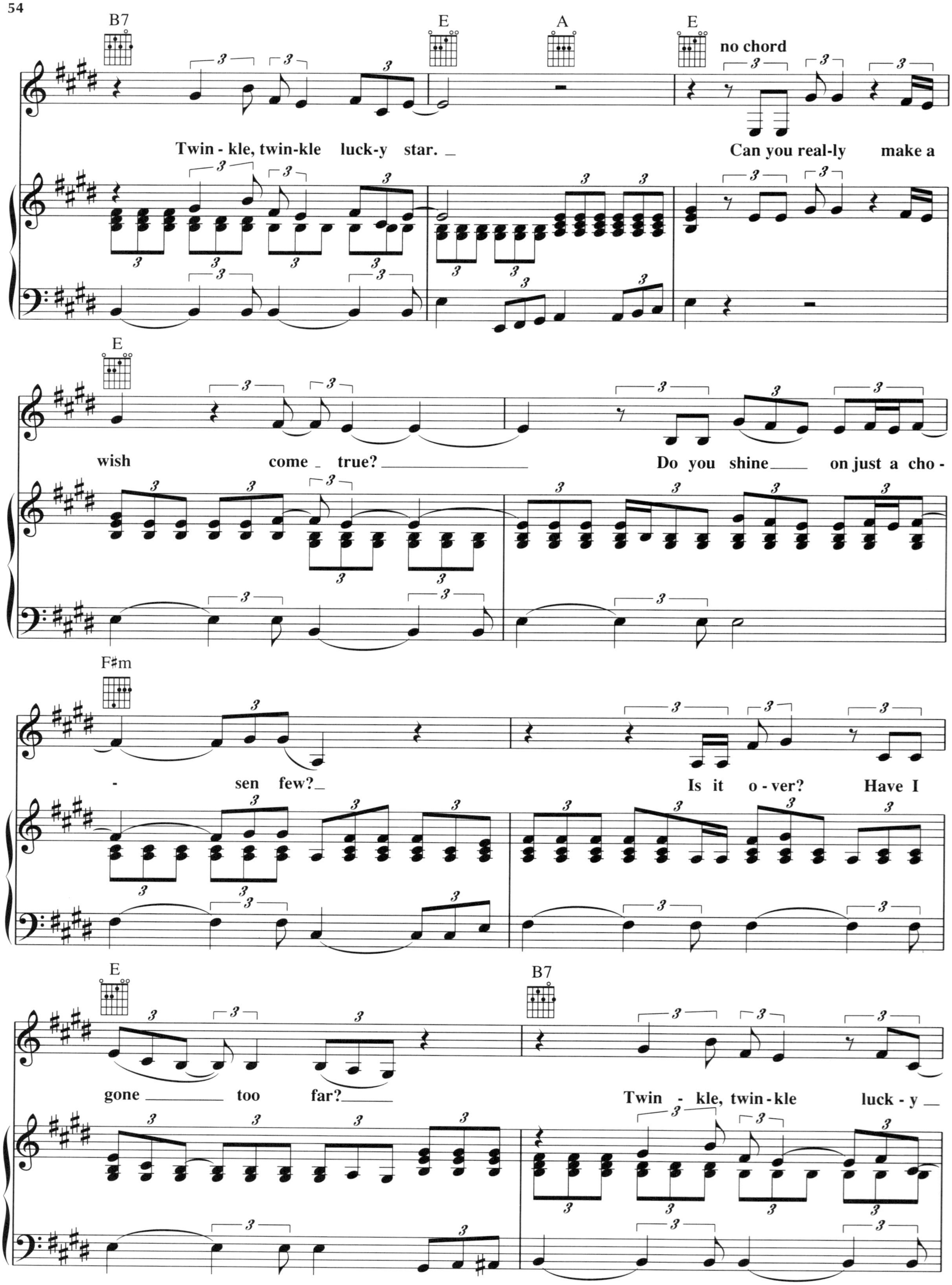
B7
E
A
E
no chord
Twin - kle, twin-kle luck-y star. _
Can you real-ly make a
E
wish come _ true?
Do you shine on just a cho -
F♯m
- sen few?
Is it o - ver? Have I
E
gone too far?
B7
Twin - kle, twin - kle luck - y _

DIXIE ROAD

Lee Greenwood

Words and Music by MARY ANN KENNEDY, PAM ROSE and DON GOODMAN

Copyright © 1980 Careers-BMG Music Publishing, Inc. and Little Jeremy Music
International Copyright Secured   All Rights Reserved

Additional Lyrics

3. Ev'ry night I'm in a diff'rent place,
And I search in ev'ry stranger's face,
Tryin' to find a girl who's just not there.
She's back there in Montgomery,
And I'm clear across the country,
But whenever I'm alone, I go back there.

CHATTAHOOCHEE

Alan Jackson

Words and Music by JIM McBRIDE
and ALAN JACKSON

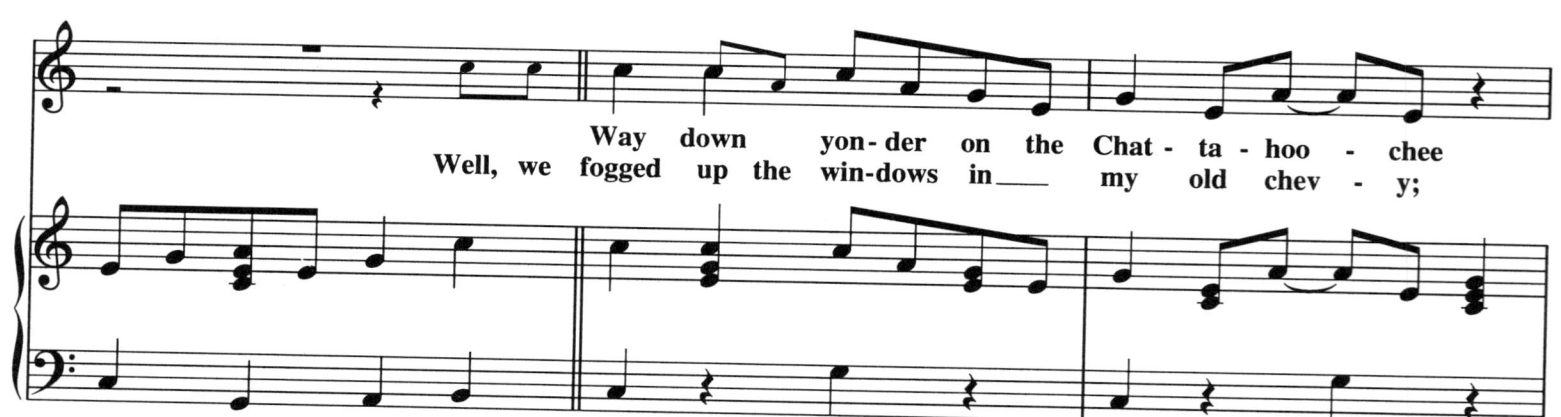

Way down yon-der on the Chat-ta-hoo-chee
Well, we fogged up the win-dows in my old chev-y;

Copyright © 1992 Sony/ATV Tunes LLC, Seventh Son Music and Mattie Ruth Musick
All Rights on behalf of Sony/ATV Tunes LLC Administered by Sony/ATV Music Publishing, 8 Music Square West, Nashville, TN 37203
International Copyright Secured   All Rights Reserved

SHE'S MY ROCK

George Jones

Words and Music by
S.K. DOBBINS

Copyright © 1972, 1975 by Famous Music Corporation and Ironside Music
International Copyright Secured   All Rights Reserved

75

Ronnie Milsap

DON'T YOU EVER GET TIRED
(OF HURTING ME)

Words and Music by
HANK COCHRAN

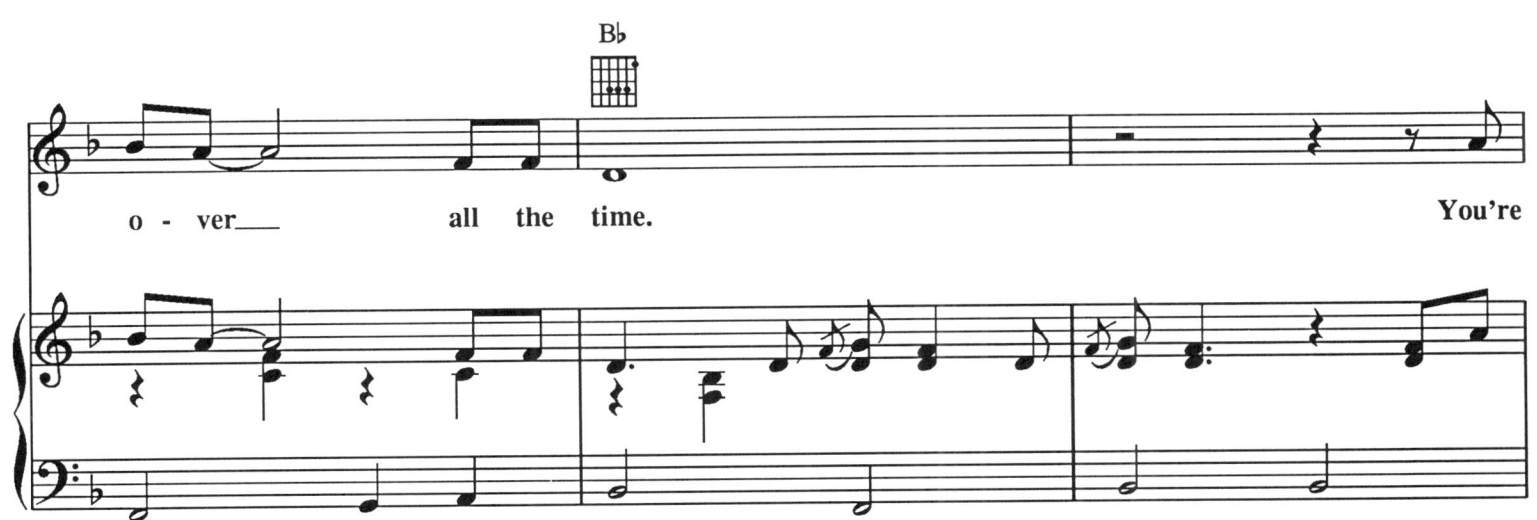

You make my eyes run o-ver___ all the time. You're

Copyright © 1964 Sony/ATV Songs LLC
Copyright Renewed
All Rights Administered by Sony/ATV Music Publishing, 8 Music Square West, Nashville, TN 37203
International Copyright Secured   All Rights Reserved

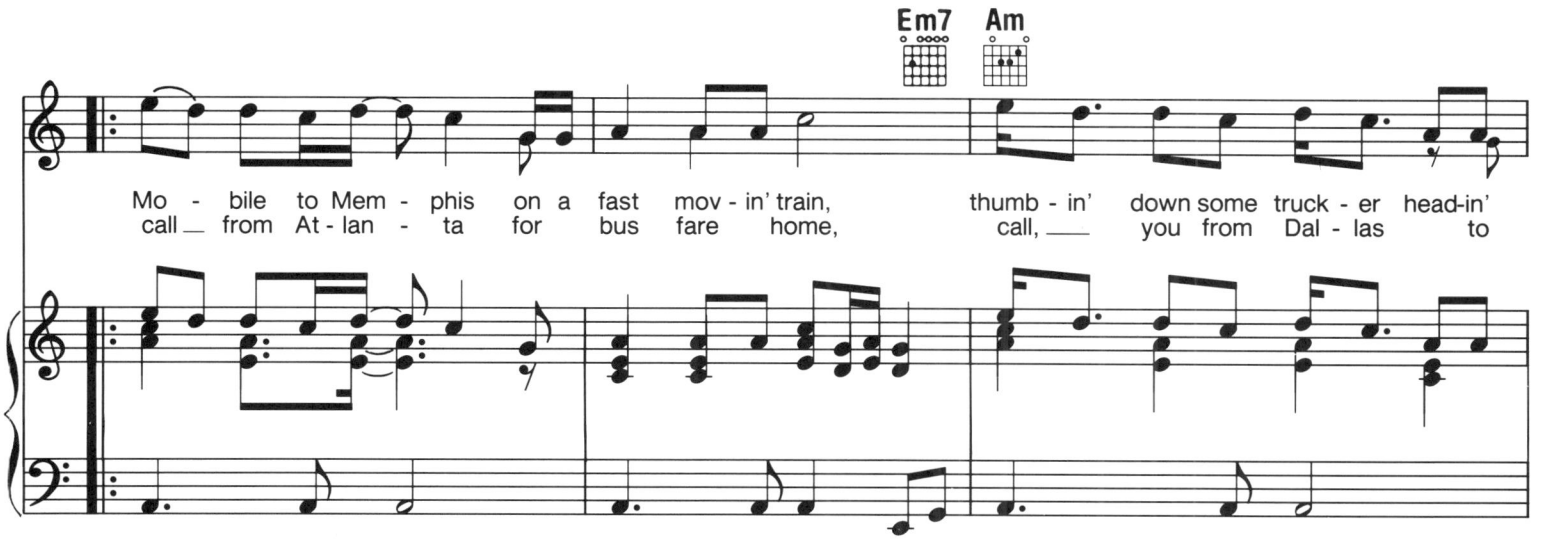
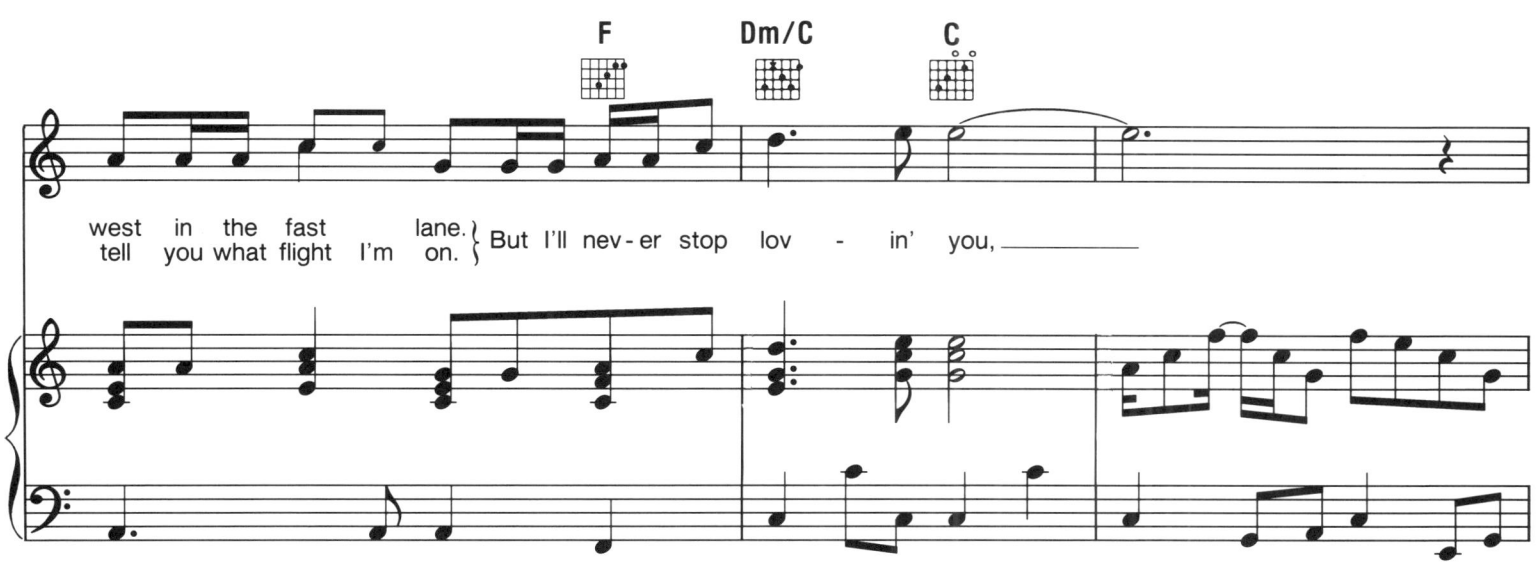
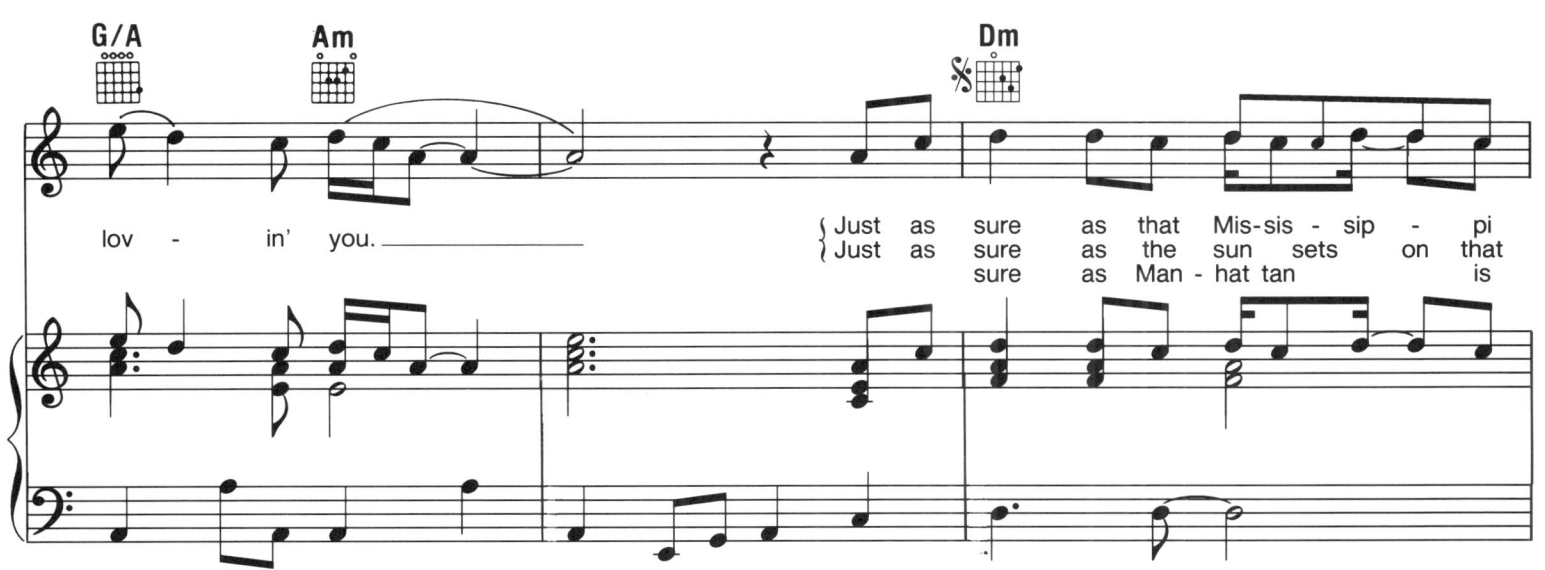

Michael Martin Murphey

WHAT'S FOREVER FOR

Words and Music by
RAFE VAN HOY

I've been look-ing at peo-ple and how they change with the times;

and late-ly, all I've been see-ing are peo-ple throw-ing love a-way and los-ing their minds.

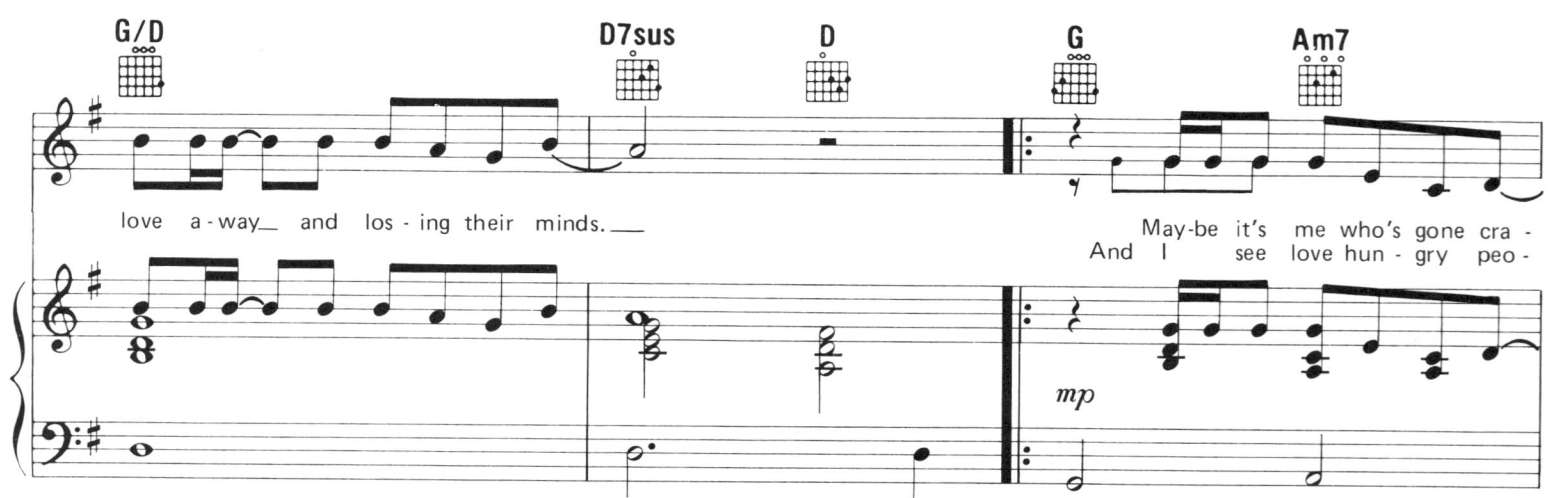

May-be it's me who's gone cra-
And I see love hun-gry peo-

Copyright © 1978 Sony/ATV Songs LLC
All Rights Administered by Sony/ATV Music Publishing, 8 Music Square West, Nashville, TN 37203
International Copyright Secured   All Rights Reserved

Additional Lyrics

2. It's been some time since she laid down the law,
   But Daddy don't seem to mind at all.
   He comes straight home when the work day's through;
   He's even done the dishes a time or two.
   Late last night when the lights were low,
   Daddy told Mama, "I love you so."
   Early this morning, Mama said to him,
   "You might just get to be a daddy again."

   Chorus

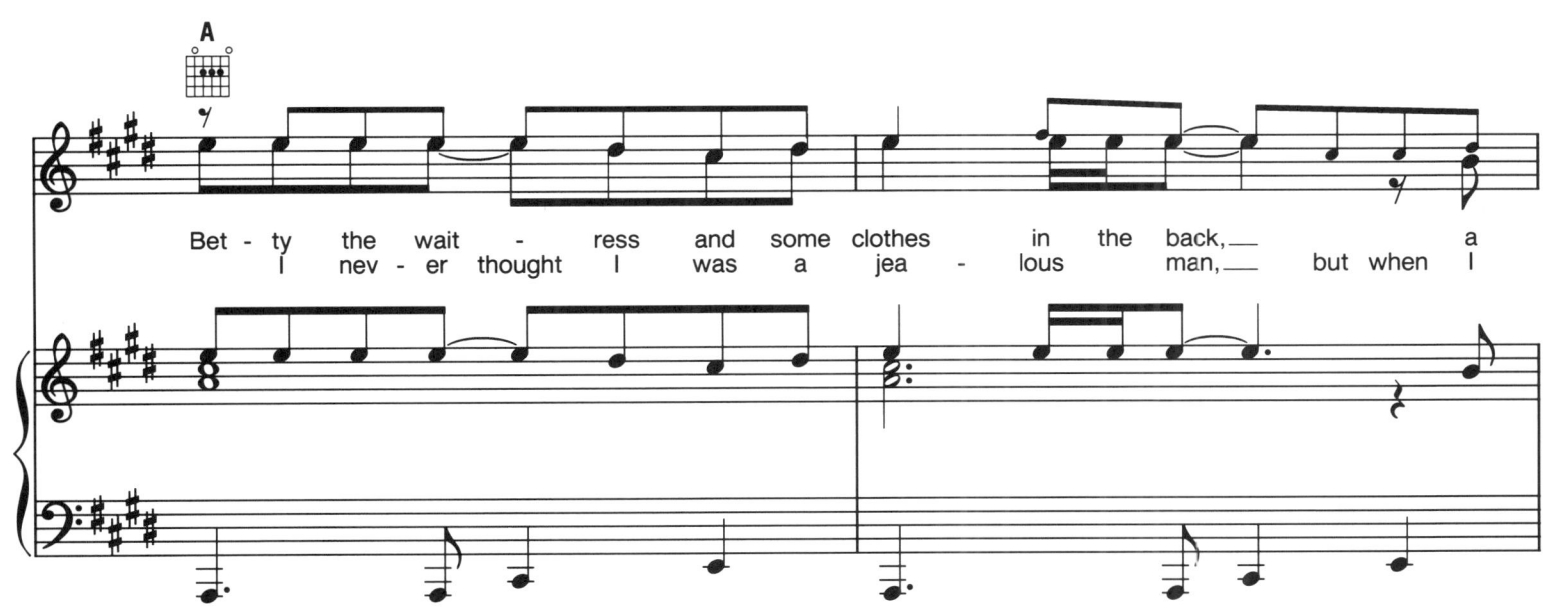

110

PARTY TIME

T. G. Sheppard

Words and Music by
BRUCE CANNEL

Moderately

Wo, — it's
par - ty time, time to get you off my mind;
par - ty time, let's have a laugh and pass the wine.
for - get the life I left be - hind and all the dreams that won't come
It's ear - ly and we're feel - ing fine;

Copyright © 1980 Sony/ATV Songs LLC
All Rights Administered by Sony/ATV Music Publishing, 8 Music Square West, Nashville, TN 37203
International Copyright Secured   All Rights Reserved

CAJUN MOON

Ricky Skaggs

Words and Music by
JIM RUSHING

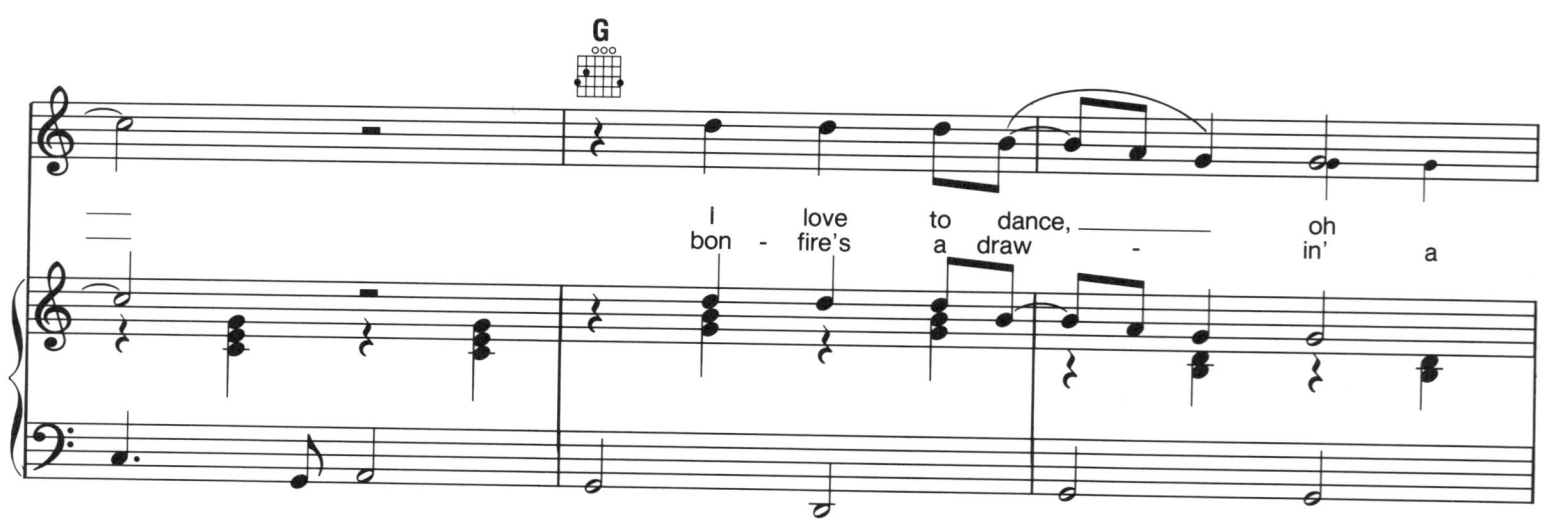

Copyright © 1985, 1986 PolyGram International Publishing, Inc. and Amanda-Lin Music
International Copyright Secured   All Rights Reserved

Additional lyrics

3. Guitar, a squeeze box, a fiddle, a bow;
   Little band a-playing every song they know.
   Old woman sittin' there and yellin' for more;
   My heart is willin', but my feet are sore.
   To Chorus

4. Once more we're waltzin' to Jolie Blond,
   I lean in closer and Sheri responds.
   Her mama's smilin' as we slip from the room
   To sit and stare at the Cajun Moon.

   To Chorus

I'LL LEAVE THIS WORLD LOVING YOU

Ricky Van Shelton

Words and Music by
WAYNE KEMP

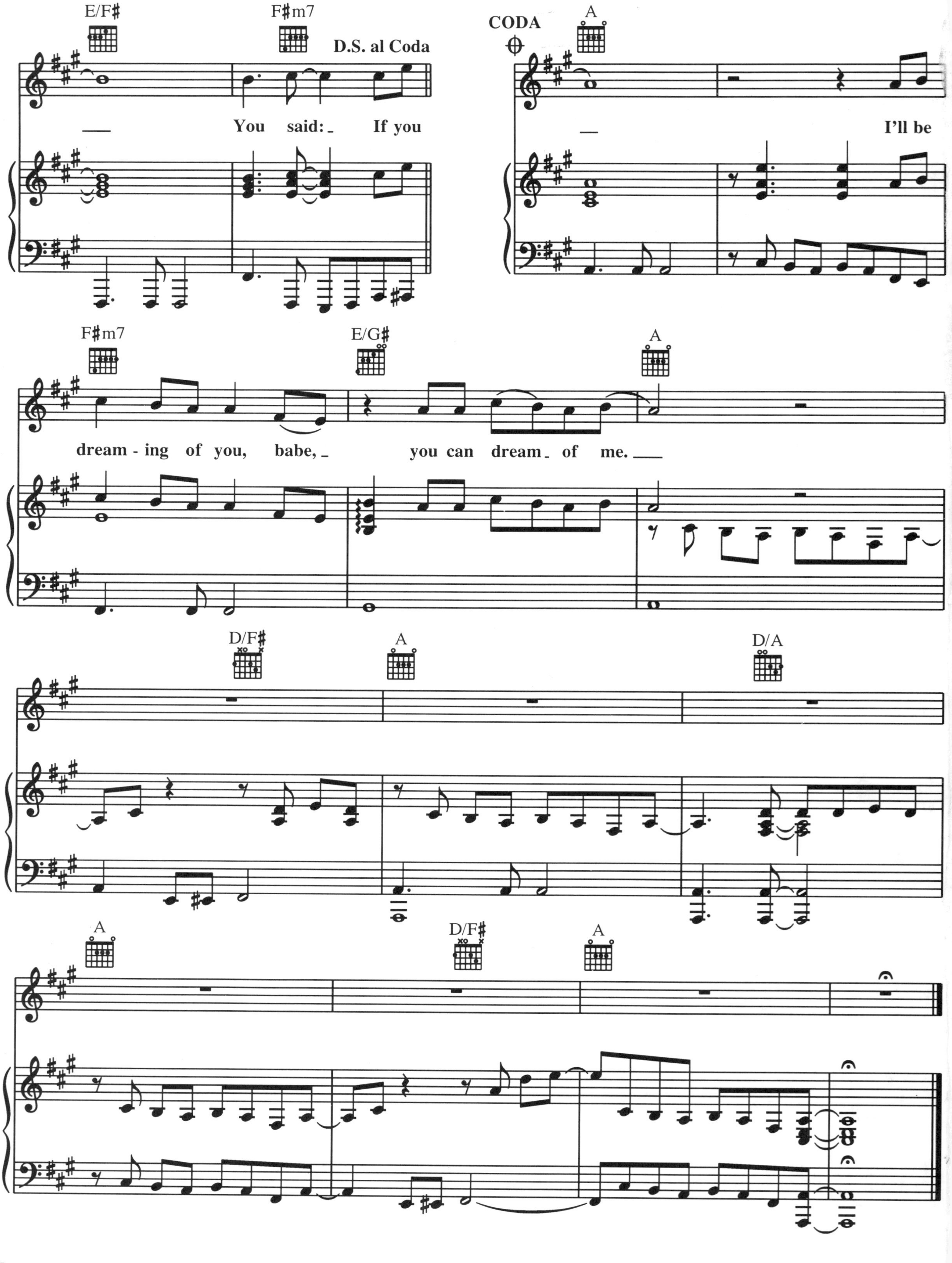
E/F♯
F♯m7
D.S. al Coda
CODA
A
You said: If you
I'll be
F♯m7
E/G♯
A
dream - ing of you, babe,
you can dream - of me.
D/F♯
A
D/A
A
D/F♯
A